THE LITTLE BOOK OF
FREEMASONRY

Written by David Greenland

THE LITTLE BOOK OF
FREEMASONRY

This edition first published in the UK in 2007
by Green Umbrella Publishing

© Green Umbrella Publishing 2007

www.greenumbrella.co.uk

Publishers Jules Gammond and Vanessa Gardner

Printed and bound in China

ISBN 978-1-905828-28-9

Contents

4 – 7	What is Freemasonry?
8 – 11	A Brief History
12 – 13	Grand Lodges and Grand Orients
14 – 17	The Lodge
18 – 21	Craft or Blue Lodge Masonry
22 – 23	Prince Hall Masonry
24 – 25	Masonic Appendant Bodies
26 – 29	Scottish Rite
30 – 33	York Rite and Royal Arch Masonry
34 – 37	Royal Ark Mariners and Other Bodies
38 – 41	Women and Freemasonry
42 – 43	Youth Organisations
44 – 47	Landmarks and Principles
48 – 51	Initiation, Oaths and Obligations
52 – 53	Degrees
54 – 61	Recognition and Regalia
62 – 69	Masonic Symbols
70 – 83	Ritual in Freemasonry
84 – 87	Masonic Myths and Conspiracies
88 – 89	Nazis and Freemasonry
90 – 91	Royalty and Prominent Freemasons
92 – 93	The Da Vinci Code

Chapter 1

What is Freemasonry?

FREEMASONRY IS THE WORLD'S oldest and largest fraternal organization with around 5 million members worldwide. It is not a secret society but is a society with secrets. The secrets of Freemasonry are mainly concerned with its traditional modes of recognition and its ritual. It is not a religion. It does not cause conflict between a man and his family or his religious beliefs. It requires that a candidate be of a certain age, is of good moral character and has belief in a Supreme Being. The Fraternity is open to men of any faith as long as they meet the other stipulations and seek to join of their own accord. Freemasonry, often shortened to Masonry, is a society of men concerned with moral and spiritual values, and is a symbol of man's search for wisdom, brotherhood and charity.

This search is ancient and is renewed every time a Lodge of Masons initiates a new brother. Through rituals, symbols and obligations, a volunteer becomes a part of a community, as he begins his own individual journey in search of 'Light'.

Its members are taught its precepts by a series of ritual dramas that follow ancient forms and use the customs and tools of 'Operative' or craftsmen stonemasons as allegorical guides. The fundamental ritual in what is called 'Speculative' Freemasonry, as practised in modern times, involves the playing out of drama that represents the building of King Solomon's Temple, and the fate of its master architect, Hiram Abif. Using this allegory, moral lessons are taught. Because the story is based on the act of building of a temple,

RIGHT The figure of
Truth, attended by
Faith, Hope and Charity
'commissioning the
genius of masonry to
illuminate the craft' in
the building of
Freemason's Hall

FAR RIGHT
The Grand Temple
inside Freemason's Hall

Masonic rituals feature the tools of stonemasons, including the level, plumb-rule, square, compasses, etc. Masonic terminology has found its way into modern language, where 'on the level' and 'on the square' are typical examples.

Freemasonry is not, in itself, a charitable organisation: its primary purpose is not the provision of charitable relief to its members. A common misconception is that it is a 'friendly' or 'benevolent' society providing financial benefits to its members in times of adversity. Charity in a Masonic sense has a much broader meaning than the giving of support to those in need. Although Masonic charity is a great fact, and is an inherent part of the Masonic system, real charity is that which is afforded by one Brother to another in the learning and understanding of Masonic truth. It embraces affection and goodwill toward all mankind, but more especially to brethren in Freemasonry. Charitable sentiment demands of the Freemason that he should 'do unto others as he would be done by', in that he would 'suffer long and be kind', be forgiving, help a Brother in need, advise him of his error and the way to put right his wrongdoing, close his ears to slander and his lips to reproach.

It is contrary to Masonic teachings that assistance in political, business or social life should be gained by one Mason from another. An approach, in furtherance of any of these, is against the principles of Freemasonry. However, a friendship formed within the Lodge may be useful in acquiring assistance in legitimate endeavours outside, but such assistance should be given as a friend, and not as a Freemason. There is nothing within Freemasonry that teaches or promotes discrimination in favour of Freemasons in any of the ordinary relationships of life, whether in business or socially.

Chapter 2

A Brief History

THERE IS SOME ARGUMENT OVER the origins of Freemasonry. It is generally accepted that there is some connection with the stonemasons who built the castles and cathedrals of medieval times but there is no absolute proof of this. Scottish Masons assert that modern Freemasonry began in Scotland in the early 1600s, when stonemasons created a system of Lodges with rituals and secrets derived from medieval mythology and Renaissance times.

The first recorded 'making' of a Freemason appears in the diary of Elias Ashmole, antiquarian and herald, whose collections were the inspiration for the Ashmolean Museum in Oxford. His diary tells of a Lodge meeting at the house of his wife's father in Warrington, Cheshire, on 16 October 1646, at which

meeting Ashmole was made a Mason: no stonemasons were present. This is the first of several records showing no connection between Freemasonry and the craft of stonemason.

Organised Freemasonry was formalised on 24 June 1717, when four London Lodges met at the Goose and Gridiron Ale House, in St Paul's Churchyard, and formed the first Grand Lodge. Initially, the Grand Lodge met annually but within four years began to meet quarterly, and soon established itself as a regulatory body. In 1723, the first rulebook, Constitutions of Masonry, was published. Grand Lodges were formed in Ireland, in 1725, and Scotland, in 1736. By that latter year, Freemasonry had grown to over 100 Lodges in England and Wales, and had spread to Europe and much of the

RIGHT Apron of a Master of the Order of the Rose-Croix

British Empire, all under control of the Grand Lodge. In 1737, Frederick, the Prince of Wales, son of King George II, was the first Royal person to be made a Freemason.

In 1751, a group of Irish Freemasons in London formed a rival Grand Lodge, claiming that the existing Grand Lodge had departed from the 'ancient landmarks', whereas the Irish claimed their Lodge to be working according the 'old institutions' granted by Prince Edwin at York, in AD926. Somewhat confusingly, the newer Grand Lodge became known as the Antients (sic) Grand Lodge, referring to the older as 'Moderns'. For more than half a century, both bodies existed independently, neither recognising the other's membership as 'regular' Freemasons.

After the French Revolution, the British Parliament passed Acts that prohibited membership of trade unions, political clubs and other subversive organisations, especially those requiring its members to take an oath or obligation. The Grand Masters of both Grand Lodges met William Pitt, the Prime Minister, and convinced him that Freemasonry upheld the principle of law and was involved in much charitable work; it thereby gained exemption from the terms of the Act.

After several years of negotiations, on 27 December 1813, the two Grand Lodges combined to become the United Grand Lodge of England (UGLE).

The UGLE established the basic administration of Freemasonry that still

a Provincial Grand Master appointed by the Grand Master of UGLE. Through the 19th century, Freemasonry grew in standing, with a high public profile largely due to the Prince of Wales (later King Edward VII) being elected Grand Master in 1874. Until the Spanish Civil War and the rise of the Nazis, Freemasonry flourished but after the Nazis banned Freemasonry, there was a marked reluctance for any publicity, and a deliberate policy of having no interaction with the media was introduced.

Resulting from this, Freemasonry began to be regarded as a 'secret' society and did nothing to refute any such claim. This situation continued until 1984: since then, the UGLE has taken positive steps to counter those claims, by adopting a policy of greater openness. Much information on Freemasonry is available to all; however, some secrets are still kept within the Fraternity.

From the original four Lodges that met in 1717, Freemasonry has grown with over 300,000 members, and more than 7,600 Lodges, in England and Wales, with a total of over 3 million worldwide.

LEFT Freemasons assemble to take part in the world record banquet, 1950

exists today. Outside London, Lodges are grouped into Provinces, based on the old counties, with each headed by

Chapter 3

Grand Lodges and Grand Orients

A GRAND LODGE, OR GRAND Orient, is the governing body of Craft or Blue Lodge Freemasonry in a particular jurisdiction. In general, Grand Lodges have control over Lodges within an area of civil government, ie English county, US state, etc.

The United Grand Lodge of England (UGLE), the Grand Lodge of Ireland, and the Grand Lodge of Scotland each govern Freemasonry within their respective countries. The UGLE also governs Lodges in Wales. Some countries within continental Europe have more than one Grand Lodge. Historically, the United States had recognised one Grand Lodge in any one state, independent of that of any other state. Today, most states have two: a mainstream Grand Lodge and a Prince Hall Grand Lodge. All mainstream Grand Lodges in the United States recognise each other; most recognise their state's Grand Lodge in Prince Hall Freemasonry (see separate section).

Grand Lodges, worldwide, function independently of any other: there is no overall ruling or governing body. Most Grand Lodges are

based on the organisation of the UGLE but are not controlled by it. Grand Lodges, and the Lodges warranted by them, are said to be in 'regularity', a process that allows formal interaction and visitation between members of different Lodges. A Grand Lodge, and any Lodge under its jurisdiction, that is 'irregular' will not be recognised, or allowed to be visited by members of any 'regular' jurisdiction. Lack of amity or irregularity, is usually due to a violation of one or more of the 25 Landmarks of Freemasonry. Although the UGLE is not an overall governing body, most Grand Lodges will consider any Grand Lodge that is, in the view of the UGLE, considered irregular, to be irregular also. Some independent bodies and Orders that are affiliated to Masonic bodies, but not governed by a Grand Lodge, generally accept the governance of that authority in their geographical area.

The Grand Orient of France is considered by all regular bodies of Freemasons to be irregular. It differs, fundamentally, from mainstream Freemasonry in that it considers a man's religious beliefs, or lack of any such belief, to be that man's business alone. Instead of a Lodge using any number of Holy Books to represent the Volume of Sacred Law, where more than one belief is represented in its membership, its Lodges may instead, use a book with blank pages. Thus, an atheist could join, without having to affirm his belief in a Supreme Being.

The head of a Grand Lodge is called the Grand Master, and the other officers of the Grand Lodge prefix "Grand" to the titles of Lodge officers. Some Grand Lodges, notably the UGLE, have established Provincial Grand Lodges as an organisational layer between themselves and member Lodges.

NDIAL DE GRANDES LOGIAS
F GRAND LODGES
SANTIAGO - CHILE MAYO 2004

Chapter 4

The Lodge

FREEMASONS MEET EITHER IN A building specifically built for the purpose of holding Masonic meetings or in a suitable hall into which the Masonic furniture is taken and then set up according to ancient tradition. The ancients were reputed to have held their Lodges outside; the teachings would take place with the Masonic images drawn in the dust or sand, and wiped away after use. More recently, Lodges were temporarily convened in buildings such as Public Houses, where 'operative' Masons would meet to plan their projects, receive their wages and socialise. Training and education would also have taken place here. Early 'speculative' Freemasons sometimes held meetings in private dwellings.

In Freemasonry, the word 'Lodge' has two meanings: it can be used in the context of a group of Freemasons meeting together, and it can also refer to the building or place in which they meet. The Lodge building is variously called a Masonic Lodge or Temple, and sometimes, Freemason's Hall. The appellation 'temple' is derived from the symbolism that Masonry uses to teach its lessons, as in the building of King Solomon's Temple in the Holy Land. The word 'lodge' is believed to originate from the name of structures built by stonemasons against the side walls of cathedrals being constructed. When bad weather prevailed, the masons had a place in which they could both shelter, or 'lodge' in, and also continue working on stones, shaping them to make them ready for use when the construction

work could continue.

A Lodge is said to be 'working' when a Lodge meeting is taking place. This working takes place according to a particular custom or 'Rite', as in Scottish Rite or York Rite (see elsewhere): the Lodge is said to be working in a particular degree, according to the standing of the membership present; this could be one of any of the three Craft degrees. All Masonic business is done in the Third or Master Mason Degree, also known as a 'regular'. None but Master Masons are allowed to be present at such meetings; balloting for candidates is generally carried out at a 'regular', as is the receiving of petitions, committee reports, and the like. The Lodge is 'opened' in the Third Degree, then formally lowered by the Master to the degree necessary for the ceremonial about to take place in that lesser degree.

No business is done in a Lodge of Entered Apprentices, except to initiate a candidate to the First Degree in Masonry, nor is any business done in a Fellow Crafts' Lodge, except to pass a Fellow Craft from the First to the Second Degree. When a candidate is initiated to the First Degree, he is styled as 'entered'. After taking the Second

Degree he is 'passed' and after he has taken the Third, he is said to have been 'raised' to the Sublime Degree of a Master Mason. No one is allowed to be present, in any degree of Masonry, unless he is of that same degree or higher. The Master always wears his hat when presiding over the Blue Lodge, but no other officer does likewise.

The Lodge, its layout and its furnishings are fundamental to the ritual; it is usually purpose-built for Masonry in order that it can follow the traditional form and layout. In some circumstances, the building utilised can be one built for another purpose, with the proviso that it can be secured and made private such that no 'cowan', a term that refers to a non-Mason, may learn any Masonic secret. The Lodge room is preferably on the first or second floor, although it is, in the First Degree, said to be the Ground Floor of King Solomon's Temple. All Lodges meet in one room, furnished in a similar manner, for the conferring of the different degrees, but it is variously called the Ground Floor, Middle Chamber and Sanctum Sanctorum (also known as the Holy of Holies) of King Solomon's Temple, according to the degree being worked.

The building may, if built for purpose, be orientated geographically in accordance with the cardinal points of the compass, but this is not absolutely necessary if the internal layout meets the criteria whereby there is a place called the 'East', for the Worshipful Master to be seated, and the other three points can be identified as North, South and West. At the West are two interconnecting rooms, one for the Tyler (or, Tiler), who guards the door to the Lodge chamber, and the other the room where an initiate is prepared for the ritual.

There is a particular layout for the Lodge room and its furniture. In the centre of the Lodge's blue ceiling is the letter 'G'. At the centre of the floor there is an altar on which there will be the Three Great Lights of Freemasonry, the Volume of Sacred Law (VSL), the Square, and the Compasses. Three candles, placed in a triangle around the altar, are known as the Three Lesser Lights, and are said to represent the Sun, the Moon and the Worshipful Master. These candles, or lights, are always lit as soon as the Lodge is opened, before the Great Lights are arranged on the altar, and extinguished after they are 'disarranged' or removed, when the Lodge is closed. There are additional items that are used in particular ritual degree conferments and ceremonial.

Officers in a Lodge form its governing body of which the highest post is that of Worshipful Master of the Lodge, who presides over Lodge affairs. Organisationally, there are usually Senior and Junior Wardens, Deacons and Stewards. Most Lodges use a similar structure, with additional appointments such as Organist, according to the requirements of the Lodge.

Business in a Lodge is carried out according to the customs and ceremonies that have existed since Freemasonry began. Some of the business activities are of a nature that anybody who has served in, or been a member of, a committee would recognise. Prior to a meeting, members are notified of the day and time of the meeting, and the agenda or order of business. After opening the Lodge in a customary ceremonial manner, the business of the day will be transacted. This may include apologies for absence, approval and signature of the minutes of the previous meeting, etc. There may also be a ceremony to confer a degree, or a study session relating to Masonry. There will be a period, usually after the meeting, when refreshments may be taken, and social interaction between members may take place.

There are two days of the year that are regarded as special, and universally celebrated in Freemasonry. Although it is a non-religious body, the feast days of St John the Baptist, on 24 June, and that of St John the Evangelist, on 27 December, are held in great regard by Masons, and duly recognised. It has been said that these two saints represent the same doctrines and values as those of Freemasons. Lodges organise events on, or around, these dates, such as ceremonial and social gatherings.

BELOW A statue of George Washington, wearing Masonic ritual garb

Chapter 5

Craft or Blue Lodge Masonry

THE CRAFT LODGE, IS ALSO known as the Blue Lodge since it has its ceiling painted in that colour. The colour blue is variously said to be traditional since "time immemorial", is the colour of the sky and is derived from a Hebrew word that can be translated as 'perfection'. Scholars of Freemasonry have found many biblical references to the colour blue in connection with Moses, as being the sacred colour of ancient priests, and a host of other possible explanations. It follows that blue is a significant colour in Freemasonry, and it is used on all manner of things connected with the Craft, particularly aprons, and collars of office.

RIGHT A general view of the ceiling of the Grand Temple inside Freemason's Hall, London

The Lodge is the recognised place where Masonry is practised, and where those seeking to join the Order will make their application. Having first passed a secret and unanimous ballot, the petitioner or candidate is notified, and presents himself for initiation. He is initiated into what is called The First Degree of Freemasonry, otherwise known as the Entered Apprentice Degree. Once initiated, in a ceremonial ritual used to confer that degree, he is called 'Brother', but is not considered to be a Mason in the full Masonic

sense. He is considered to be a rough 'ashlar', in Masonic language a rough stone, ready to receive guidance and assistance. This is achieved through the appointment of a mentor, usually a Learned Brother, by the Lodge. The mentor assists the Entered Apprentice to reach the level of proficiency required to advance to the next degree in the Masonic hierarchy.

The Entered Apprentice receives tools that were used by the ancient craftsman in his work of erecting a building. These tools are symbolic in the shaping of man in his behaviour to society and community. In the Entered Apprentice degree, these tools are the Twenty-four-inch Gauge and the Common Gavel: the gauge is a passive tool, used for measurement and calculation and the gavel is used actively, and represents force. While in this degree, the Entered Apprentice has the right to sit only in the Lodge in which he received his degree, and when the Lodge is open in that degree. He has the right to advancement after satisfactorily passing an examination in open Lodge. He cannot vote or hold office. He may, with consent of the Master of the Lodge, visit another Lodge open in the same degree, if accompanied by a Master Mason who has sat with him in open Lodge, and can vouch for him.

The Second Degree in Freemasonry, the Fellow Craft Degree, is that in which an Entered Apprentice is initiated in order that he might receive more 'Light'

the work they raised was perpendicular; in Freemasonry, it teaches a man to be upright before God and man. The square teaches the need to square our actions in virtue, while the level symbolically reminds us of the level of time, in which all men travel on a one-way journey, and from where there is no return.

The Master Mason, or Third, Degree, is said to be the height of Ancient Freemasonry, and also the most sublime. As in the two previous degrees, it allows the initiate, when properly prepared and vouched for, to receive more Light in Masonry. He receives the tools of the Master Mason that includes all the tools from the previous degrees and, in addition, the trowel: traditionally used by stonemasons to spread the cement used to bind a building together; it is a symbol used for the purpose of spreading Brotherly Love.

Lodges are said to be open in any one of the three degrees. A Mason can only enter a Lodge when it is open in the degree into which he has been duly initiated. Lodge business is carried out when it is open in the Third Degree; when initiating an Entered Apprentice, it is lowered to the First Degree.

LEFT Freemasons gather at Earl's Court for the 25th anniversary of the formation of the Premier Grand Lodge

in Masonry. It requires that he has become proficient in the First Degree, and is properly vouched for by another Brother. In this degree, the initiate receives the symbolic tools of the Plumb, Square, and Level. The plumb was used by stonemasons to ensure that

Prince Hall Freemasonry

PRINCE HALL FREEMASONRY (PHF), otherwise known as 'Black Masonry', is named after a freed, former African slave, Prince Hall who, in 1775, was made a Mason, along with fourteen other former slaves, by an Irish Military Lodge. In 1784, the Grand Lodge of England granted a charter to African Lodge No 459, in Boston, Massachusetts, with Prince Hall as its first Worshipful Master.

After a period in which no dues were received, the African Lodge was struck off the Register of Lodges by the Grand Lodge of England in 1813. However, the Lodge continued under Prince Hall, and began to charter other Lodges. In 1827, it declared itself independent, and became a Grand Lodge, chartering other black Lodges across the United States.

PHF operates in a manner that Freemasons would recognise. Each Lodge confers three degrees and there is a similar dress code of dark suit and shoes, black socks, white shirt and dark tie, that is strictly enforced. Lodge rooms are similar to those in most other Lodges, with the main difference being that the Master sits in the East under a canopy supported by two columns. The Lodge and Grand Lodge organisational structure is

LEFT Count Basie

BELOW Sugar Ray Robinson

similar to that of other bodies.

On petitioning a Prince Hall Lodge, an investigating committee is appointed. Each Candidate has to learn a catechism. Although the vast majority of PHF Masons are of African ethnic origin, there is no barrier against a white Caucasian or person from any other ethnic origin, petitioning for admission; similarly, there are black members of some mainly white lodges in other, non-PHF, Masonic bodies. On becoming a Master Mason, he can petition either the York or Scottish Rites, become a Shriner or join the Order of the Eastern Star.

Many prominent black Masons from the world of entertainment and elsewhere are, or were, Masons of the PHF, including notables such as Edward Kennedy 'Duke' Ellington, Nat 'King' Cole, Count Basie, Sugar Ray Robinson, Booker T Washington, and the Reverend Jesse Jackson.

Today, Prince Hall Freemasonry has about 275,000 members, mostly black, while other Freemasonry organisation memberships are mostly white. Most of its Lodges are in the United States, with a Grand Lodge in each state. There is at least one PHF Lodge in Great Britain.

PHF is the largest body of black Masons and its warrant and standing is recognised by other Masonic organisations; however, there are several smaller 'clandestine' groups that have broken away from PHF, and have set up their own bodies. Among these, are: the International Masons, the Fitzpatrick Grand Lodge and the Grand Lodge of Enoch. None of these are recognised by the PHF, neither is there any communication with any of them.

Chapter 7

Masonic Appendant Bodies

THE HIGHEST DEGREE IN CRAFT or Blue Lodge Masonry is that of Master Mason. However, there are a number of organisations related to Freemasonry that are known, variously, as 'appendant', 'affiliated', or 'concordant' bodies, otherwise, bodies 'in amity'. Among these are the Scottish Rite* and the York Rite* (*see elsewhere); both admit only Master Masons to their organisation. Additionally, there are some bodies, including the Order of the Eastern Star and the Order of the Amaranth, that admit both Master Masons and non-Masons who have some family relationship to a Master Mason. Other affiliated bodies, mainly in Youth Organisations* (*see elsewhere), such as the Order of DeMolay and the International Order of the Rainbow for Girls, are open to non-Masons, with no requirement for any relationship to a Master Mason. There are Orders that require a member to be of a specific religion, an apparent conflict with the ideals and principles of Freemasonry, or those having previously held a specific office in a Masonic body or an affiliated group.

Following the merger of the two Grand Lodges in 1813, it was agreed that pure 'Antient' Masonry consisted of the three degrees of Entered Apprentice, Fellow Craft and Master Mason, and none other. However, following discussions over the semantics of the

ABOVE A depiction of a ritual taking place in a masonic lodge, New York, circa 1900

agreement, several other degrees were admitted. Prior to 1813, there had been an emergence of a great many Masonic rites, often with new rituals that widened the scope of Freemasonry, as well as those rituals previously practised in Craft Masonry. Some of these rites died out, often without any documentary proof they were ever practised, while others survived the merger of the two Grand Lodges.

Not all Masonic jurisdictions recognise these appendant bodies: some formally recognise them, while others consider them to be totally outside of Freemasonry.

Chapter 8

Scottish Rite

THE SCOTTISH RITE IS THE COMmon name for The Ancient and Accepted Scottish Rite of Freemasonry (AASRF), and is one of several Rites of the worldwide fraternity of Freemasonry. Contrary to its name, the Rite is not actually Scottish, having originated in France, where its degrees were based on legends brought from Scotland by Masons fleeing from the unrest and persecution during the 17th and 18th centuries.

Scottish Rite has existed formally since 1801, when the Mother Supreme Council was formed in Charleston, South Carolina. This Council is officially titled "'The Supreme Council (Mother Council of the World) of the Inspectors General Knights Commander of the House of the Temple of Solomon of the Thirty-third

Degree of the Ancient and Accepted Scottish Rite of Freemasonry of the Southern Jurisdiction of the United States of America." Known colloquially as the Southern Jurisdiction, all regular Scottish Rite bodies are derived from this body. The AASRF Northern Jurisdiction was formed in 1813. Each country's body is headed by a Supreme Council, that of England and Wales receiving its warrant from the Northern Jurisdiction of the USA in 1845.

In England and Wales, Scottish Rite is officially titled 'The Ancient and Accepted Rite for England and Wales and its Districts and Chapters Overseas' but is known informally as the Rose Croix. In England and some other countries, the Scottish Rite is not officially recognised by the Grand Lodge, but there is no barrier to a

Master Mason electing to join it. In the USA, however, the Scottish Rite is officially recognized by Grand Lodges as an extension of the degrees of Freemasonry. In New Orleans and some other areas, the Scottish Rite versions of the three Craft or Blue Lodge degrees are conferred.

The Scottish Rite builds upon the ethical teachings and philosophy offered in the Craft or Blue Lodge, through dramatic presentation of the individual degrees and, for that reason, is sometimes known as the College of Freemasonry. All Scottish Rite jurisdictions worldwide, operate independently; as a result, there are variations in their respective degree systems. Each local body, a 'Valley', confers degrees from

the Fourth to Thirty-second at degree-conferring meetings. The Thirty-third degree is an honorary award for outstanding service to the Order or, in life.

LEFT Certificate of the High order of the Freemasons of 33rd rite in Scotland written in German, 31st May 1913

Degrees of the Ancient and Accepted Scottish Rite:

4°	Secret Master
5°	Perfect Master
6°	Intimate Secretary
7°	Provost and Judge
8°	Intendant of Buildings
9°	Master Elect of Nine
10°	Master Elect of Fifteen
11°	Sublime Master Elected
12°	Grand Master Architect
13°	Royal Arch of Enoch (formerly of Solomon)
14°	Grand Elect, Perfect and Sublime Master Mason
15°	Knight of the East or Sword
16°	Prince of Jerusalem
17°	Knight of the East and West
18°	Knight of the Rose Croix de Heredom
19°	Grand Pontiff
20°	Grand Master of all Symbolic Lodges
21°	Noachite or Prussian Knight
22°	Knight of the Royal Axe
23°	Chief of the Tabernacle
24°	Prince of the Tabernacle
25°	Knight of the Brazen Serpent
26°	Prince of Mercy

27°	Commander of the Temple
28°	Knight of the Sun
29°	Knight of St Andrew or Patriarch of the Crusades
30°	Knight Kadosh
31°	Grand Inspector Commander
32°	Sublime Prince of the Royal Secret
33°	Inspector General

Four coordinating bodies, each under a presiding officer, administer degree levels within jurisdictions:

	(Northern)	(Southern)
Lodge of Perfection	4° to 14°	4° to 14°
Chapter, Rose Croix	15° & 16°	15° to 18°
Council of Kadosh	17° & 18°	19° to 30°
Consistory	19° to 32°	31° & 32°

While the Masonic apron in Craft or Blue Lodge is descended from the medieval stonemason's working apron, the distinctive Scottish Rite Mason's cap, along with his other regalia, is inherited from the full dress regalia of medieval European orders of chivalry. On receiving the Thirty-Second Degree (32°), and donning the black satin headgear of the Scottish Rite, the Master Mason craftsman is elevated to an order of Masonic knighthood. Other chivalric accoutrements denote rank or office of the wearer within the Order.

Chapter 9

York Rite and Royal Arch Masonry

THE YORK RITE, OTHERWISE known as the American Rite (sometimes, Canadian Rite), is based on the Craft Masonry practised in the early 1700s. When the first Grand Lodge of England was formed in 1717, it specified that Lodges were to confer only the three degrees of Entered Apprentice, Fellow Craft and Master Mason, and none other. Some Lodges considered the Royal Arch to be an integral part of Masonry, so they formed their own breakaway Grand Lodge in 1751, and continued to confer the Royal Arch. After the formation of the United Grand Lodge of England in 1813, it was agreed that only the prescribed three degrees would be conferred by Lodges,

RIGHT A meeting of a branch of the Knights Templar

but the Royal Arch would be attached to Chapters affiliated to Lodges. Attainment of the Royal Arch degree is fundamental to Freemasonry, and is the climax of Masonic symbolism. It is the duty of each Master Mason to complete the degree: without it, the Masonic character is not complete.

The York Rite comprises a grouping of three separate Rites or Chapters that are joined in order: Royal Arch (Capitular), Royal and Select Masters (Cryptic) and Knights Templar (Chivalric). Unlike the Scottish Rite, degrees within the York Rite are not numbered.

The Royal Arch Chapter, which is the first order to be joined by a Master

Mason, confers the following degrees: Mark Master, Past Master, Most Excellent Master and Royal Arch Mason. It has been said that "The Royal Arch stands as the rainbow of promise in the Ritual; it stands as the promise of the resurrection of that which was lost and that which shall be recovered."

Mark Master is probably the oldest Masonic degree, and one of the most highly respected, teaching practical lessons for everyday living. It is believed to have been based on the ancient ceremony of registering a masonry craftsman's 'mark' to distinguish his work in temple building. In England, and some countries in Europe and Australasia, the Mark degree is conferred on a Master Mason in a separately warranted Lodge of Mark Masters. A Council of this Lodge may also confer the degree of Royal Ark Mariner. In Scotland the Mark degree is conferred in a Craft Lodge or, in exceptional cases, in a Holy Royal Arch Chapter. The Holy Royal Arch degree is similar to that of the Royal Arch in the York Rite but is considered a separate Order.

The Past Master degree teaches the important duties and responsibilities of

A Knight Templar in his military

f the XIV Century

habite

the Oriental Chair, and is a qualification for advancement. Only those of this degree can receive the Royal Arch degree. The Most Excellent Master degree is considered the most spectacular degree in Freemasonry, teaching the fundamentals for the completion and dedication of King Solomon's Temple.

The Royal Arch degree teaches the story of the time in Jewish history when Jerusalem and the Holy Temple were destroyed, and its people held captive in slavery in Babylon. It tells how some of the slaves returned to their homeland, and rebuilt Jerusalem and the Temple, during which they discovered the Master's Word. After attaining the Royal Arch degree, the Freemason may either continue to take Cryptic Masonry degrees of: Royal Master, Select Master, Most Excellent Master (in Great Britain) and, optionally, Super-Excellent Master or, may proceed directly to Knights Templar. Admission to the Order of Knights Templar requires that the Master Mason promises to defend the Christian faith. Knights Templar has three degrees: Illustrious Order of the Red Cross, Order of the Knights of Malta (or simply Order of Malta) and Order of the Temple.

Chapter 10

Royal Ark Mariners and Other Bodies

THE ANCIENT AND HONOURABLE Fraternity of Royal Ark Mariners, more commonly known as RAM or Mariners, has been under the jurisdiction of the Grand Lodge of Mark Master Masons since 1871, and is governed by the Grand Masters Royal Ark Council. It relates to the building and voyage of Noah's Ark and the Great Flood, and has none of the other characters that exist in Freemasonry. Origins are believed to relate to carpenters and woodworkers, who worked alongside stonemasons in ancient times. The degree ceremonial is carried out in a curious non-rhymed metre, axes are used instead of gavels and aprons are of undressed leather instead of the more usual lambskin. RAM Lodges are attached to Mark Lodges under the host Lodge's number and name, unless dispensation for variance be given by the Grand Master.

As previously stated, there are many other bodies associated with Freemasonry, either by affiliation to the mainstream 'Rites' or by the requirement of a recognised Masonic degree to be held by a prospective member. Membership of some of these bodies is by invitation only, a practice contrary to the principles of Freemasonry.

The Royal Order of Scotland confers two degrees: Heredom of Kilwinning, which explores the symbolism of the Craft degrees of Masonry, and The Rosy

RIGHT Star symbol

Cross, originally for Scottish Masons only, which is effectively a 'Knighthood' for services rendered by a Brother of Heredom. Membership of the Order is by invitation only to Master Masons of five years' standing, and there may be other restrictions.

An organisation called the Allied Masonic Degrees (AMD) exists in both England and the United States, and is centred around Masonic research and scholarship. Membership is by invitation only, and is open to Companions who have completed Chapter degrees in bodies known as Councils, under a National Grand Council. The internal Council structure, officer titles and ritual are similar to those of Craft, or Blue, Lodges. The English body works the five degrees, the last four being taken in any sequence: St Lawrence the Martyr, Knight of Constantinople, Grand Tilers of Solomon, Red Cross of Babylon and Grand High Priest. The American body works around ten degrees, some of which have the same names as in the English counterpart.

The Societas Rosicruciana in Anglia is not a Masonic Order, but requires those joining to be Christian and a Master Mason. It differs from Masonry in that it uses 'Grades' rather than degrees, and has its own officer rank titles, including: Supreme Magus, Chief Adept, and Suffragan. The Order explores the mystical and symbolic side of Masonry.

The Order of the Eastern Star is the largest fraternal organisation in the world, with over one million members, that is open to both men and women. Based on teachings from the Bible, it is open to all who acknowledge a Supreme Being. Members must be 18 years or older, men must be Master Masons, while women must have a specific relationship, ie originally either wife, daughter, sister, mother or widow, to a Master Mason. Other women may now be admitted, and the Order allows Rainbow Girls, and Job's Daughters (see Youth Organisations) to join when they become of age.

The Order of the Amaranth has similar criteria for membership as those of the Eastern Star, and teaches the values of truth, faith, wisdom and charity, along with their duties to God, their country and fellow beings.

Chapter 11

Women and Freemasonry

WOMEN WERE ADMITTED INTO the fraternity long before Freemasonry was officially recognized. The forming of the United Grand Lodge of England effectively put a stop to this, however, declaring in 1717 that women were not to be admitted into the craft. There were still women masons after that point, but no more were admitted and eventually, only men were left. The "Ancient Landmarks" that the Grand Lodge of England assembled as being the basic tenets of the fraternity, effectively put a stop to further women's admission.

It is claimed that the first woman Freemason was the daughter of one of the workmen building King Solomon's Temple. Each day, she brought his lunch and watched him working, and asked if she could try to cut the stone. He showed her how to shape the stone, and soon she became proficient at the craft. The overseer, Hiram Abif, brought her before an assembly of the workmen and insisted she be initiated as Entered Apprentice. After the ceremony a mason, named Adoniram, confronted Hiram with the claim that, since time immemorial, only men had been so initiated, and the act was against the ancient Landmarks. Hiram replied with the assertion that God had given her the skill to become a mason; he (Hiram) had only given her the means to improve herself in Masonry.

Another story tells of how in 1712,

Elizabeth Aldworth, a girl from Cork, Ireland, was found eavesdropping on a Lodge meeting in her father's house. The brethren of the Lodge agreed that she be initiated through the degrees, to ensure her secrecy. She lived the true life of a Mason, eventually becoming Master of the Lodge.

Modern women's Freemasonry came to England in 1902, when Annie Besant, who had been initiated into a French mixed order called Le Droit Humain, established a Co-Masonic Lodge in London. Over the years, the Co-Masonic movement spread, becoming more in line with regular men's Freemasonry in that the founder brought about change, since known as the Annie Besant Concord, that recognised the existence of God or a Supreme Being, a tenet missing from the origins in French Freemasonry of Le Droit

Humain. Eventually, in 2001, the Grand Lodge of Freemasonry for Men and Women was Constituted and Warranted.

An organisation founded in 1908, known as the Honourable Fraternity of Ancient Freemasonry was originally a mixed body but, in 1918, after the deaths of its remaining male membership, became an exclusively women's organisation. It has since become known as the Order of Women Freemasons (OWF), with a membership of over 1,000 women. The Order currently comprises just over 350 Craft Lodges, based in the British Isles,

Australia, Canada, Malta, Zimbabwe and also southern Spain.

Other organisations exist that are open to, or exclusively for, women. Among these are the Order of the Eastern Star, the Order of the Amaranth, the White Shrine of Jerusalem, the Social Order of Beauceant and the Daughters of the Nile. Women Freemasons follow similar ceremonies and practices as their male counterparts, even to the extent of calling each other "brother", although some bodies use the term 'sister'. The United Grand Lodge of England has, in 1999, acknowledged the regularity and sincerity of women's Freemasonry, although it is does not officially recognise it.

Chapter 12

Youth Organisations

THREE MAIN YOUTH ORGANISA-tions are affiliated to Freemasonry, but are separate and independent from it. They all stress the importance of character development, community service and leadership. While members of the youth groups are free to seek membership in Freemasonry, or bodies such as the Eastern Star, it is a matter for personal choice, and is not a requirement for membership.

Perhaps the best known, the Order of DeMolay is an organisation for young men aged from 13 to 21 years. It is not a prerequisite for a prospective member to have a Masonic relative. Founded in the United States in 1919, it is now an international body, with Chapters in several countries. The International Order of Rainbow for Girls, known as Rainbow Girls, is an organisation for young women aged 11 to 20 years, and was founded in the United States in 1922. As for the DeMolay, no Masonic relationship is required for member-ship. Taking its name from a Biblical story in the Book of Job, the International Order of Job's Daughters was founded in Nebraska, USA, in 1920. Membership is for young women aged between 11 and 20 years who are related to a Mason.

In the early 20th century, the leader of Scouting in New Zealand, Major David Cossgrove, started a scheme named The Empire Sentinels, that would cater for boys when they became too old to remain as Boy Scouts. Documentation exists that appears to confirm that the Sentinels held many of the same principles as Freemasonry.

RIGHT Freemasons' seal

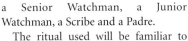

The scheme was structured around three Watchtowers, and three degrees of efficiency: based on religious duty, with proof of the ability to work, of patriotism and good citizenship and better work, self-sacrifice in service to others and still better work. Officers were to be: a Chief Sentinel, a Sentinel of the South, a Sentinel of the East, a Sentinel of the West, an Inner Guard, an Outer Guard,

a Senior Watchman, a Junior Watchman, a Scribe and a Padre.

The ritual used will be familiar to Masons: "The Tower is opened in the 3rd Watch, then dropped to the 2nd or 1st as required. Sentinels enter using a pass word, and saluting." It describes how "Halters and blindfolds are used," and tells how the 'Alarm' appears to be the same number of knocks as the Watch in which the Tower is working. The Masonic saying, 'So Mote it Be', is mentioned. There are four principal officers in the Tower ceremonies, and the Chief Sentinel sits in the North. Lights are lowered, and symbols of office illuminated, in each Watch.

While there is no evidence that Baden-Powell, founder of the Scout movement, was ever a Mason, he held Masonic principles in high regard. Members of his family, including his brother, were active Freemasons. In Australia, people actively connected with the Scout movement in that country formed a Lodge named The Baden-Powell Lodge. Lord Baden-Powell inscribed the Lodge Bible when he visited Australia in 1934.

Chapter 13

Landmarks and Principles

IN ANCIENT TIMES, LANDMARKS were pillars of stone, denoting boundaries. This definition has been perpetuated, by many Masonic writers, by the use of the term in describing the fundamental principles under which Freemasonry is constituted. There can be no deviation from these 25 'Antient (sic) Landmarks'; neither can they be altered by adding to or taking from them. Landmarks are, effectively, cast in stone.

1. The Modes of recognition.
2. The division of Symbolic Masonry into three degrees.
3. The legend of the third degree.
4. The government of the fraternity by a presiding officer called a Grand Master.
5. The prerogative of the Grand Master to preside over every assembly of the craft.
6. The prerogative of the Grand Master to grant dispensations for conferring degrees at irregular times.
7. The prerogative of the Grand Master to grant dispensation for opening and holding Lodges.
8. The prerogative of the Grand Master to make Masons on sight.
9. The necessity of Masons to congregate in Lodges.
10. The government of every Lodge by a Master and two Wardens.
11. The necessity that every Lodge,

when duly congregated, should be tyled (guarded).

12. The right of every Mason to be represented in all general meetings of the craft and to instruct his representatives.

13. The right of every Mason to appeal from the decision of his brethren in Lodge convened, to the Grand Lodge or General Assembly of Masons.

14. The right of every Mason to visit and sit in every regular Lodge.

15. That no visitor, not known to some

brother present as a Mason, can enter a Lodge without undergoing an examination.

16. That no Lodge can interfere in the business of another Lodge nor give degrees to brethren who are members of other Lodges.

17. That every Freemason is amenable to the laws and regulations of the Masonic Jurisdiction in which he resides.

18. That every candidate for initiation must be a man, free born and of lawful age.

19. That every Mason must believe in the existence of God as the Grand Architect of the Universe.

20. That every Mason must believe in a resurrection to a future life.

21. That a book of the law of God must constitute an indispensable part of the furniture of every Lodge.

22. That all men, in the sight of God, are equal and meet in the Lodge on one common level.

23. That Freemasonry is a secret society in possession of secrets that cannot be divulged.

24. That Freemasonry consists of a speculative science founded on an operative art.

25. That the Landmarks of Masonry can never be changed.

However, not all jurisdictions accept, or authorise, all of these Landmarks; some use variations on the wording of individual Landmarks. The main points of controversy are: Landmark 3, some disagree that the three Craft degrees are a Landmark, Landmark 8 is not agreeable to some, Landmark 14, some jurisdictions consider 'visiting' to be a privilege, not a right and Landmark 20 raises theological questions that cannot be addressed.

The following Five Points of Fellowship are fundamental principles within the Order of Freemasonry:

1. When the necessities of a brother call for my support, I will be ever ready to lend him a helping hand to save him from sinking, if I find him worthy thereof.

2. Indolence shall not cause my footsteps to halt, nor wrath to turn them aside, but, forgetting every selfish consideration, I will be ever swift of foot to save, help and execute benevolence to a fellow-creature in distress, but more particularly to a brother Mason.

3. When I offer up my ejaculations to Almighty God, I will remember my

brother's welfare, even as my own, for as the voice of babes and sucklings ascends to the throne of grace, so, most assuredly, will the breathings of a fervent heart ascend to the mansions of bliss.

4. A brother's secret, delivered to me as such, I will keep as I would my own, because, if I betray the trust which has been reposed in me, I might do him an irreparable injury; it would be like the villainy of an assassin, who lurks in darkness to stab his adversary when unarmed and least prepared to meet an enemy.

5. A brother's character I will support in his absence, as I would in his presence. I will not revile him myself, nor suffer it to be done by others, if it is in my power to prevent it.

Thus, by the five points of fellowship, Freemasons are linked together in one indivisible chain of sincere affection, brotherly love, relief and truth. A Mason receives the secret of the Five Points of Fellowship along with the real grip or handshake, during the ritual for the Master Mason's degree.

Chapter 14

Initiation, Oaths and Obligations

IN FREEMASONRY, THE TERM initiation can be interpreted in several ways. In practical terms it is said to be the first stage of the journey from Darkness into Light: initiation into the Order is only the beginning of a man's journey in search of Light. He then gains further wisdom as he progresses through the degrees of Masonry, on a path in search of knowledge and self-fulfilment.

A candidate must, in the first instance, make an application, or petition, to a Lodge. This must be made of his own volition; it is contrary to the principles of Freemasonry for any Mason to coerce or influence a candidate into joining the movement.

The basic requirements for any candidate are: that he should be a man, freeborn, of good repute and well-recommended, have belief in a Supreme Being, be able to support his family, be of lawful age and come to Freemasonry of his own free will and accord.

When his application is received, the Lodge begins a process that will investigate the candidate, to find out if he is both of good character and is a sincere applicant. The investigation may take some time as part of the process is to ascertain whether the candidate is prepared to wait patiently; a virtue regarded as being essential in the life of a Mason. The Lodge may appoint an examining committee of members to carry out the actual investigation.

In some jurisdictions, there is an informal meeting with a candidate, usually on neutral ground, where he can feel at ease, and they may get to know each other, and talk over aspects of Freemasonry. This process may vary between jurisdictions, as each Grand Lodge can set its own rules and procedures for the investigation. There must be confirmation that the candidate is of the required minimum age and, in some cases, he

must have been known to a member of the Lodge for a given time. It may be that, after several meetings, an investigating member may conclude that a candidate is suitable for Masonry, and offer to sponsor him. Investigation is a very serious and solemn process: if a candidate subsequently becomes unfit for membership, then the sponsor would be placed in a difficult situation;

therefore, due diligence will be exercised to ensure the candidate meets all of the necessary criteria for admission to Freemasonry.

Questions may be asked by the applicant about the Lodge meeting times, dress code, joining and ongoing membership fees, and any other points on which he may seek clarification. Every opportunity will be taken to

ensure that the prospective member is fully aware of the implications of Freemasonry, so that he can form a judgement on whether he should proceed further. When the investigating committee's report is returned to the Lodge, a ballot of members will be taken: the result of the ballot

must be unanimous in acceptance of the candidate. If successful, the candidate is notified of the date and time to present himself for initiation.

During initiation, and on other occasions during his life as a Mason, there will be the requirement to make obligations under oath. Outsiders may have some awareness of so-called 'Bloody Oaths' taken by Freemasons. Most people on the outside have been told, or may have read about the implicit consequences of breaking an oath, and of the consequent, apparently barbaric, punishments that are said to be carried out. In the Order, lessons are taught using allegory, whereby a particular aspect is shown, often by practical means, in the acting-out of play dramas, in a way that may not be easily understood using only the spoken word. At all stages, the candidate is reminded that any obligation he is about to make will not, in any way, interfere with any duty or obligation to God, his family and friends or himself.

While there may have been some evidence in history to the contrary, the 'Bloody Oaths' made in modern Freemasonry are symbolic only, and allegorical in nature. The only penalties that can be imposed on an errant Mason are: reprimand, suspension or expulsion; these being imposed according to the severity of the wrongdoing.

On learning of the apparent imbalance between the punishment meted out, in cases where one or more of the oaths have been broken, and the terminology of the actual oath, it can be argued that oaths are unnecessary: a member of any organisation who breaks its rules would leave himself open to similar sanctions, depending on the severity of his transgression. In Masonry, the oaths and obligations taken by a member are taken as an indication of his sincerity and commitment to the Order, and his fellow brethren.

Chapter 15

Degrees

THE ARTICLES OF UNION BET-ween the two Grand Lodges of England were signed on 25 November 1813 by the Duke of Sussex and the Duke of Kent, and confirmed on 27 December 1813 prior to the constitution of the United Grand Lodge of England: Article II "...declared and pronounced that pure Antient Masonry consists of three degrees and no more, viz., those of the Entered Apprentice, the Fellow Craft, and the Master Mason, including the Supreme Order of the Holy Royal Arch."

Masonry uses symbols and plays, as in medieval times, to teach the great lessons of life. Each degree represents attainment of a particular stage in the development of a Freemason. In Craft or Blue Lodge Masonry, there is no degree higher than that of Master Mason. However, some Masonic bodies,

known as Concordant or Appendant Bodies, exist with further degrees

RIGHT Masonic temple detail

having higher numbers. These higher degrees are considered as supplemental to the degree of Master Mason, rather than superior. One example is the Scottish Rite (see 'Scottish Rite' section), that confers degrees numbered from 4° up to 33°. Appendant or Concordant bodies each have their own organisational structure, similar to that of Craft or Blue Lodge Freemasonry except, in some areas, notably in North America and Canada, where there are three

Scottish Rite bodies, the Canadian Jurisdiction, Southern Jurisdiction and the Northern Jurisdiction, which have slightly different titles for their degrees.

The York Rite (sometimes called the American Rite) has a different organisational structure (see 'York Rite' section). In some countries, the Grand Lodges will have degree systems based on variations of either the York Rite or Scottish Rite degrees. Freemasons working through the degrees often prepare papers on related philosophical topics and often present these in open Lodge. Their topics may range from organisation, performance of rituals and Masonic history.

Terminology in Freemasonry, with regard to the appellation of a member, has a logical relationship to every stage in the hierarchical degree structure. When a candidate receives the First Degree he is said to be 'initiated', at the Second Degree he is 'passed', at the Third, 'raised' and when he takes the Mark Degree, he is 'congratulated' (advanced). Having passed the chair, he is said to have 'presided', when he becomes a Most Excellent Master, he is 'acknowledged and received' and when a Royal Arch Mason, he is 'exalted'.

Chapter 16

Recognition and Regalia

HANDSHAKES OR 'GRIPS', SIGNS and gestures are used as a means of recognition between Freemasons. Grips were originally used by the ancient stonemasons as a means of recognition both by day and by night. Special grips were used by these masons, as they moved between jobs, to identify themselves as being of a high rank or standing within their craft; hence, the need for the grips to be kept secret to prevent others from usurping the status of the craftsman. Similarly, in modern Freemasonry, different grips, signs and gestures are used to recognise others, and to distinguish between members of different degrees: as in ancient times, these grips are required to be kept secret, not only from outsiders but also those who may be of a lower degree, ie an Entered Apprentice (of the First Degree) is not privy to grips, signs or gestures used within the degrees of the Fellow Craft (Second Degree) or the Master Mason (Third Degree).

The secret sign or 'duegard', gesture, and grip (handshake) are only made known to the candidate for Freemasonry during the actual ceremonial ritual for that particular degree. This prevents a Mason becoming privy to information that is above his station in the Craft. The duegard is used as a salutation to the Worshipful Master of the Lodge and, in the degree of Entered Apprentice, is represented by standing

with forearms parallel across the body, and with palms facing each other, as though supporting the Holy Book on the left hand, and with the right hand resting thereon, as if taking an oath. The sign of the Entered Apprentice is made by drawing the right hand rapidly across the neck in a cutting motion, then dropping the hand rapidly to the side, symbolising the act of having "…my throat cut across, my tongue torn out by its roots and my body buried in the rough sands of the sea at low water mark, where the tide ebbs and flows twice in twenty-four hours, should I ever knowingly violate this my Entered Apprentice obligation." The handshake or grip of the Entered Apprentice, is made by pressing the thumb against the top of the first knuckle-joint of the fellow Mason, the fellow Mason also presses his thumb against the first Mason's knuckle. The name or pass (word), of this grip is 'Boaz'.

The duegard of the Fellow Craft represents the positions of the hands when taking the oath of the Fellow Craft degree: "…my right hand on the Holy Book, square and compasses, my left arm forming an angle, supported by the square and my hand in a vertical position."

The Fellow Craft sign is made by cupping the right hand over the left breast, drawing it quickly across the body, then dropping the hand to the side, alluding to the penalty for breaking the oath or

as the 'pass grip', as the Entered Apprentice receives the Second Degree, and is made by pressing the top of the Fellow Craft's thumb against the space between the first and second knuckle joints of the first two fingers of his fellow Mason; the fellow Mason also presses his thumb on the corresponding part of the first Mason's hand. The pass name of this grip is "Shibboleth". He then receives what is called the 'real grip' in which the Mason takes the fellow Mason by the right hand as in an ordinary hand shake and presses the top of his thumb hard on the second knuckle, the fellow Mason presses his thumb against the same knuckle of the first Mason's hand. This grip is called 'Jachin'

The duegard of the Master Mason alludes to the position of the hands when taking the oath of the Master Mason: "both hands resting on the Holy Book, square and compasses." The sign of the Master Mason is made by drawing the thumb quickly across the waist to the right hip, then dropping the hand to the side. This action shows the stomach being ripped open, symbolically alluding to the penalty of the Master Mason's obligation: "…to have my body cut in two, my bowels removed and burned to

obligation of the Fellow Craft degree that refers to "…having my left breast torn open, my heart plucked out, and given to the wild beasts of the field and the fowls of the air." The first grip of the Fellow Craft degree is known

RIGHT Masonic
handshake

ashes which are then to be scattered to the four winds of heaven." The pass grip of the Master Mason has the name "Tubalcain", in which the Mason places his thumb on the space between the second and third knuckles of the fellow Mason's right hand, while the fellow Mason moves his thumb to the corresponding space on the first Mason's hand. The thumb is pressed hard between the second and third knuckles of the hands.

In the real grip, the Master Mason firmly grasps the right hand of a fellow Mason. The thumb and fourth finger grasp around the wrist of the other Mason while he presses the tops of his fingers, held slightly apart, against the wrist of the fellow Mason where it unites with the hand; the fellow Mason does the same. This grip is called "Ma-Ha-Bone", and is known as the Strong Grip of the Master Mason or, the Lion's Paw. The name of the grip is passed to the Mason during the ritual in which he is 'raised' or resurrected, in accordance with the legend of Hiram: the Worshipful Master symbolically raises the Mason from the dead by offering his hand in the grip, and raises him to the position known as the Five Points of Fellowship. This position is demonstrated as the Worshipful Master and candidate embrace one another while standing; foot to foot, knee to knee, breast to breast, hand to back and cheek to cheek or mouth to ear. While in this position, and at low breath, the Worshipful Master then whispers "Mah-Ha-Bone" into the ear of the candidate. "Mah-Ha-Bone" is the substitute for the Master's Word. It means, "What, the Builder!" In the obligation or oath of the Master Mason he says: "Furthermore, I do promise and swear that I will not give the substitute for the Master's Word in any other way or manner than that in which I receive it, which will be on the Five Points of Fellowship, and at low breath."

After he becomes a Master Mason, the candidate receives instruction on the Grand Hailing Sign of Distress: it is given by raising both hands toward heaven, with each arm forming the angle of a square, or a 90 degree angle. The arms are then lowered in three distinct motions to the sides, ending with both arms in the natural downward position. The candidate is additionally instructed that, if he is in a place where the sign could not, or should not be seen, he is to utter a substitute for the sign: "O Lord, my God, is there no help for the Widow's Son?" He is additionally advised that the sign, and these words, are never to be given together, and also swears: "Furthermore, I do promise and swear that I will not give the Grand Hailing Sign of Distress of a Master Mason, except for the benefit of the Craft while at work or for the instruction of a Brother, unless I am in real distress, and should I see the sign given, or hear the word spoken, I will hasten to the relief of the person so giving it."

For the purpose of attending a Lodge, a strict Masonic dress code is imposed on members: for men, a dark or black suit, black shoes and socks, white shirt and black tie; women wear a black suit, or trouser-suit, with a white blouse. Over the suit is worn the Masonic Regalia, which primarily consists of an apron with a flap at the top denoting the degree or rank of the member. The apron is worn with the flap turned up to denote the First Degree, the flap turned down but one apron corner turned up and tucked into the apron string, in the Second Degree. In the Third Degree, the apron is worn with the flap and corners turned down, as worn by the ancient master stonemasons. The apron reflects the leather apron worn by the stone masons in ancient times to protect themselves from the stone being worked; modern aprons are made from either lambskin, leather, silk or plastic. Apron size is stipulated by the Masonic body governing the Lodge; it is usually sized around 15 inches by 17 inches (38cm by 42cm). The apron must be worn to be readily visible.

A yoke collar is used as a badge of office in Freemasonry, and is usually embroidered with the insignia of the Order or degree of the wearer, and may carry a pendant badge of office known as a jewel. Jewels are also worn as a breast brooch, and are generally made of either gold, silver or base metal, with the design portrayed in coloured enamel. Sashes also form part of the distinctive regalia, as do white cuffs and gloves. Freemasons usually carry their regalia and jewels in a purpose-designed briefcase.

LEFT Masonic hand-crafted detail

Chapter 17

Masonic Symbols

A SYMBOL IS DEFINED IN THE Oxford English Dictionary as being "a thing that represents or stands for something else." The American Heritage Dictionary defines symbol as being "something that represents something else by association, resemblance or convention, especially a material object used to represent something invisible." In Masonry, the symbolism of a specific sign, object, number or word, is not for the lowly Craft Mason to fully understand, and will be revealed only when he becomes a 32° or 33° Sublime Prince of Freemasonry. Furthermore, the Craft or Blue Lodge Mason is apparently, and intentionally, misled as to the true meanings of some of these symbols. In a book, Morals and Dogma, written by Albert Pike, a pre-eminent authority on Freemasonry, he writes (on page 819):

"The Blue Degrees are but the court or portico (porch) of the Temple. Part of the symbols are displayed there to the initiate, but he is intentionally misled by false interpretations. It is not intended that he shall understand them, but it is intended that he shall imagine that he understands them… their true explication (explanation and understanding) is reserved for the Adepts, the Princes of Masonry (those of the 32nd and 33rd Degrees)."

Most people are familiar with the sign used outside a Masonic Hall or Temple, consisting of the square and compasses, surrounding the letter 'G'. Each of these individual items or symbols can have more than one meaning, depending on the circumstance of its use in Masonry. For example, the letter 'G' can represent 'Geometry', and was held sacred by the

Pl. 1.

Est

Nord

Sud

B   J

Ouest

Tracé
de la Loge d'Apprenti

ancient Pythagoreans: it can also represent the initial letter of the name of the Earth Goddess Gaia. In ancient scripts, the 'G' was represented thus Γ, having similar form to the Mason's square. The letter is also used to denote God. Compasses were used in Operative Masonry to measure the architect's plans, and transfer these into proportions in the work: in Speculative Masonry, the compasses are symbolic of rectitude and virtue. The square was used by the stonemason to measure the precision of angles on stones to ensure the perpendicularity of his building; in Freemasonry it represents accuracy, integrity and rightness in character. It is also the badge of office of the Worshipful Master of the Lodge.

RIGHT The Three Great
Lights of Freemasonry

Two pillars within the Lodge room represent those at the entrance to King Solomon's Temple. Some Masonic symbols are worked onto a carpet in the room, known as the Master's Carpet. Three Steps symbolically represent the three principal stages of human life: youth, manhood and age. Three Columns are emblems of Wisdom (of Solomon), Strength (of Hiram, King of Tyre) and Beauty (Hiram Abif, the widow's son). The Pot of Incense is an emblem of a pure heart. The Beehive is an emblem of industry, and recommends the practice of that virtue to all created beings. The Book of Constitutions, guarded by the Tyler's Sword, reminds a Mason to be watchful and guarded in thoughts, words and actions, particularly when before the enemies of Masonry. The Sword pointing to a Naked Heart demonstrates that justice will sooner or later overtake us. The All Seeing Eye beholds the inmost recesses of the heart, and will reward us according to our works. The Anchor and Ark are emblems of a well-grounded hope and a well-spent life.

An invention of Pythagoras, The Forty-Seventh Problem of Euclid, the theorem of the square on the hypotenuse of a right angled triangle, teaches Masons to love arts and sciences. The Hour-glass is the symbol of human life: as the sand runs away, so does life. The Scythe is an emblem of time, and cuts the thread of life, sending us into eternity. The Spade will dig our grave; the Setting-maul (a heavy hammer, represented by a padded buckskin bag in Masonic ritual) that ended the life of Hiram Abif, may end ours, also. The Coffin receives our remains, the Grave that may soon be ours and the Acacia is the symbol of faith in the immortality of our soul. Masonic ritual is, in itself, symbolic.

The Lodge is said to have 'Ornaments' and 'Jewels'. The Ornaments are: the Mosaic Pavement that represents the Ground Floor of King Solomon's Temple, with a Blazing Star in the centre, and The Indented Tessel, the beautiful border that surrounds it. The six Jewels of the Lodge are three 'movable' jewels: the rough ashlar, the perfect ashlar, and the trestle-board (on which the lessons are taught). The immovable jewels are the Square, Level, and Plumb.

Symbolism is not confined to objects

having form: numbers, letters and words have symbolic meanings within Freemasonry. At the heart of Masonry, is the ancient Greek and Hebrew concept of Gematria, which involves reading words and sentences as numbers, assigning a numerical, instead of a phonetic value, to each letter of the Hebrew alphabet. When read as numbers, they can be compared and contrasted with other words. The symbolism of sacred numbers prevails throughout Freemasonry. Originally attributed to followers of Pythagoras, it was probably of earlier Egyptian or Babylonian origin, who believed that all things proceeded from numbers. In the Pythagorean system, odd numbers were considered to be symbols of perfection: in Freemasonry, although other 'even' numbers may have some significance, the sacred numbers are all odd numbers: 3, 5, 7, 9, 15, 27, 33, and 81.

In Masonry, the number 3 relates both to the Three Great Lights of Freemasonry (namely, the Volume of the Sacred Law (Holy Book), the Square and the Compasses), and also the three most symbolic of the five human senses, those relating to seeing, hearing and touching, by virtue of their importance in Masonic recognition and ritual. The number 5 is of great importance throughout Freemasonry, symbolising the number of steps in the middle section of the Lodge room's 'winding stairs' that represent the five human senses and the five orders of architecture. The five points of fellowship and the five-pointed star, together with Geometry, also known as the fifth science, all serve to show the importance of the number. Similarly, the number 7 has great significance as representing the number of years it took to complete King Solomon's Temple, which was dedicated to the glory of God in the seventh month, and the ensuing

festival that lasted seven days.

Some numbers are either symbolic in themselves, or are multiples of those having symbolic status, as in 27, which is the number 3 'cubed'. Similarly, the number 81 is a multiple of 9. Other numbers, although not sacred, have great significance in Masonry; the number 4 was considered by the Pythagoreans to be a perfect number and, in Freemasonry, it is the degree number of Perfect Master. It also represents the number of letters in the spelling of the name of God in many ancient civilisations, and is the name of the Jews in Tetragrammaton, with its four Hebrew letters usually transliterated as YHWH or JHVH, pronounced Jehovah, used as a biblical proper name for God. It also represents the four sides of a square in geometry, a perfection.

Hiram Abif (or Abiff) is a symbolic character in Freemasonry. The Order maintains that Hiram was the principal architect at the building of King Solomon's Temple. The legend of Hiram in Freemasonry is said to be based on a biblical story, wherein King Solomon invited another Hiram, King of Tyre, to provide materials and manpower to construct a Temple. A specially gifted craftsman was needed to lead the project: a 'Widow's Son', Hiram Abif, was sent, and became chief architect, a Master of Geometry.

The skills of the Temple builders were considered both secret and sacred, given by a God who loved mankind and wanted a man to be able to take care of his family. Skills varied from that of the beginner or apprentice, the next being that of craft mason and the highest that of a craft master: these skill levels are reflected in modern Craft Masonry as the Entered Apprentice, the Fellow-Craft and the Master Mason.

Hiram Abif, Solomon, King of Israel, and Hiram, King of Tyre, are the three most exalted personages in the Masonic world. They are believed to have knowledge of the secrets of a Master Mason, either inherited, or invented by them: these secrets were not to be divulged to any other person without the mutual consent of all three. Three craft masons at the Temple, Jubela, Jubelo and Jubelum, known in Masonic tradition as the Ruffians, sought to obtain knowledge of the secrets and approached Hiram. When he refused, they killed him in a manner described in Masonic ritual, breaking his skull with a setting-maul.

LEFT Grave with masonic symbol

Chapter 18

Ritual in Freemasonry

RIGHT A large crowd watches the installation of a Grandmaster

OVER THE CENTURIES, FREE-masonry has passed on its teachings, in closed Lodge, to successive generations of men who seek the Light. Its lessons are passed on to each new Freemason, and to those seeking further Light in the degrees, by the use of allegory, in which the story is told in the form of play dramas, carried out in the 'theatre' of the Lodge. In particular, the ritual used in the degree ceremonials has been used with little or no change for several hundred years. A Mason from any juris-diction, in any country, would recognise the ritual being performed as being the same as that practised in his own Lodge.

A duly constituted Lodge in any of the three degrees usually requires a quorum of seven brother Masons in the Lodge room, and the Tyler at the Outer Door. However, the Fellow Craft Lodge need only consist of five, and the Master Masons' Lodge, only three. It is the Tyler's duty to ensure that all brothers arriving at the Lodge are made aware of the degree in which the Lodge is work-ing, in order that no cowan, or outsider, may overhear any of the ritual; neither may any member who is not of the same, or higher, degree than that being worked. This protects the secrecy of the higher degree's duegard, signs and grips.

At a Lodge meeting, the brethren gather before the scheduled time at the Lodge room, which has been furnished, usually by the Tyler. At the hour of meeting, the Worshipful Master (WM) takes his place at his seat in the East, puts on his hat, sash, yoke and apron, and with gavel in hand says: "Brethren will be properly clothed and in order; officers repair to their stations for the

purpose of opening." At this announcement the brethren put on their aprons, officers their yokes also, and seat themselves around the Lodge room.

Officers take their stations: Senior Warden (SW) in the West, Junior Warden (JW) in the South, Senior Deacon (SD), with his long rod of office, in front of, and slightly to the right hand side of the WM in the East, Junior Deacon (JD) at the right hand of the SW in the West, guarding the inner door of the Lodge, with rod in hand, Secretary forward, and to the left of the WM, and Treasurer forward and to the right. Usually, there are two Stewards one on either side of the JW in the South, with rods in hand. After all are seated, the WM says: "Is the Tyler present? If so, let him approach the East."

At this command the Tyler, who has remained near the Outer Door that is used by brothers of the Lodge, approaches the WM, wearing his yoke and apron. A dialogue ensues in which the WM asks the Tyler of his duties; namely, to keep cowans, profane, and eavesdroppers at bay, and allow only those duly qualified to enter. The Tyler receives his sword of office, and retires to his place outside the Inner Door, that connects the Lodge room and Ante-room. All Lodge doors are then closed, upon which the WM gives one rap of his gavel to bring the JD to his feet, and then questions him as to whether he is aware of his duty, to see that the Lodge is duly tyled. The JD then opens the Inner Door and verbally gives the Tyler

the degree of working, then closes the door and gives the appropriate number of raps for that degree; there is a similar response from the Tyler. The JD then informs the WM that the Lodge is duly tyled, by a properly qualified member of the degree, in possession of his sword of

RIGHT A one dollar bill depicting a truncated pyramid and the all-seeing eye

office, and with instructions to keep out all cowans, 'Morgans' (book-learned Masons), and eavesdroppers. He then returns to his seat.

The ritual proceeds with one rap of the WM's gavel. The SW rises to his feet, and, in ritual dialogue between the WM

and SW, confirms that all present are of the required degree, and that the SW was duly initiated into this Lodge. Further questions from the WM to the SW regarding the number present, and the officers' places in the Lodge. The WM then questions each officer in turn as to his duties, and also asks of the place in the Lodge, and the duties of the next officer. The final questions are to the SW as to the WM's station in the Lodge, to the East, and his duty there. His reply: "As the sun rises in the East, to open and govern the day, so rises the Worshipful Master in the East (here the SW gives three raps with his gavel, upon which he, and all the brethren of the Lodge, rise), to open and govern his Lodge, set the craft to work, and give them proper instructions."

The WM then says: "Brother Senior Warden, it is my orders that this Lodge be opened on the (Number) Degree of Masonry (usually the Third Degree – then, lowered to a lesser degree, as necessary). For the dispatch of business during which time, all private committees, and other improper, un-masonic conduct, tending to destroy the peace of the same while engaged in the lawful pursuits of Masonry, are strictly forbid-

RIGHT Old door with
Freemasonry symbol

den, under no less penalty than a majority of the brethren present, acting under the by-laws of this Lodge, may see fit to inflict: this you will communicate to the Junior Warden in the South, and he to the brethren around the Lodge, that they, having due and timely notice, may govern themselves accordingly."

The SW then says to the J W in the South: "Brother Junior Warden, you have heard the orders of the Worshipful Master, as communicated to me from the Worshipful Master in the East. You will take notice, and govern yourself accordingly." The JW addresses the Lodge, saying: "Brethren, you have heard the orders of the Worshipful Master, as communicated to me through the Senior Warden in the West. You will please take notice, and govern yourselves accordingly."

The WM says the words: "Brethren, together on the signs" (or, sign, if open in the First Degree), whereupon the Master leads off, in the giving of the signs of the three degrees. If the Lodge is open in one of the first two degrees, then only those signs are given, first the duegard, then the sign, of each degree in turn. The brethren respond with the same duegard and sign. In the Third Degree, the Grand Hailing Sign of Distress is also given. After the signs, a series of gavel taps from the Master and each of the Wardens, one tap for each degree of working, is made three times, before the Master removes his hat and repeats the following part of the Scripture: "Behold, how good and how pleasant it is for brethren to dwell together in unity! It is like the precious ointment upon the head, that ran down upon the beard, even Aaron's beard, that went down to the skirts of his garments, as the dew of Hermon, and as the dew that descended upon the mountains of Zion: for there the Lord commanded the blessing, even life forever more." Amen! To which the brethren respond: "Amen! So mote (sic) it be!"

The Master then declares the Lodge open in the particular degree, and instructs the JD to inform the Tyler. This done, the WM calls upon the SD to attend at the altar, and places the square over the points of the compasses, if in the First Degree. In the Second Degree, one point is placed on top of the square and, in the Third Degree, both points are on top.

In raising or lowering the degree of the Lodge, ritual ceremonial is performed in order that only those who are properly qualified remain in attendance. This takes the form of an individual enquiry of those present, as to the 'pass' word and sign belonging to that degree. When a Lodge is being raised in degree, for example, to the Third Degree for Lodge business, then those who are of a lower degree will not know the pass sign in response to the enquiry, and will be required to leave the Lodge room. Formal Lodge business is also carried out in ritual, particularly in the ballot for admission of a new member.

During the initiation of a candidate, a specific ritual ceremonial takes place; the ritual is somewhat different for each degree, but similar in the manner in which it is performed. For an Entered Apprentice, the ceremony begins after the Lodge has been duly opened, then lowered, to the First Degree. The candidate waits in the Ante-room, to where the JD and his assistants, two Stewards and the Secretary come to prepare him. Prior to him being readied, the Secretary interrogates the candidate to ascertain that his application was made voluntarily, and he has no ulterior motive for becoming a candidate for

Masonry. The Secretary returns to the Lodge to report satisfactory replies have been made. The candidate is then readied for initiation. There is some variation on the description given here, but the essence remains the same.

The candidate is now requested to take off his coat, shoes, stockings, vest and cravat, if worn. Historically, a pair of long drawers was given, but it is more usual for the candidate's own trousers to be worn, the left leg rolled up above the knee. The left arm is pulled from the sleeve, so that the arm and breast are bared. The JD ties a blindfold, a hoodwink, over the candidate's eyes, places a slipper on his right foot, and places a rope in the form of a slack noose, called a cable-tow, around the neck with the free end hanging loose. There is some variance on the position of the noose. In the Fellow Craft or Second Degree, the right arm and breast, and the right knee, are bared, and the slipper placed on the left foot, with the cable-tow wound twice around the right upper arm. The Master Mason Degree requires both arms and the breast, both knees, and both feet, to be bared, and the cable-tow is wound three times around the body. All candidates

are fitted with the hoodwink.

The JD now takes the candidate by the arm, leads him forward to the door of the Lodge, and gives three distinct knocks. A dialogue ensues in which the JD, speaking for the candidate, says: "Mr (Name), who has long been in darkness, and now seeks to be brought to light, and to receive a part in the rights and benefits of this worshipful Lodge, erected to God, and dedicated to the Holy Saints John, as all brothers and fellows have done before."

A dialogue then follows in which the SD asks the JD if the candidate is here of his own accord, properly qualified, and vouched for, and is a free man of good repute. The candidate is instructed to wait patiently until the WM is informed, and gives his reply. The SD closes the door and proceeds to the altar, where he raps once on the floor with his rod, and receives a similar reply from the WM with a rap from his gavel.

The dialogue that took place at the door is repeated whereon the WM says: "Let him enter, and be received in due form." The SD removes the compasses from the altar, moves to the door and opens it, and repeats the words of the WM. Then, the SD steps backward, the JD and the candidate enter the Lodge, followed by the Stewards. As they enter, they are stopped by the SD who presents one point of the compasses to the candidate's left breast, and says: "Mr (Name), on entering this Lodge for the first time, I receive you on the point of a sharp instrument pressing your naked left breast, which is to teach you, as it is a torture to your flesh, so should the recollection of it ever be to your mind and conscience, should you attempt to reveal the secrets of Masonry unlawfully. In the Fellow Craft Degree, the angle of the square is used, and its meaning given; in the Master Mason Degree, both points of the compasses are pressed against the breasts.

The JD leaves the candidate in the care of the SD, and retires to his seat. The SD, followed by the two Stewards, proceeds to lead the candidate once around the Lodge room by taking him by the right arm, advancing by a step or

two until the WM raps once with his gavel, then they stop. The WM says: "Let no one enter on so important a duty without first invoking the blessing of the Deity. Brother Senior Deacon, you will conduct the candidate to the centre of the Lodge, and cause him to kneel for the benefit of prayer." The SD instructs the candidate to kneel, then the WM leaves his seat and kneels by the side of the candidate at the altar, and says a prayer: "Vouchsafe Thine aid, Almighty Father of the Universe, to this our present convention, and grant that this candidate for Masonry may dedicate and devote his life to Thy service, and become a true and faithful brother among us! Endue him with a competency of Thy divine wisdom, that, by the secrets of our art, he may be better enabled to display the beauties of brotherly love, relief and truth, to the f Thy Holy Name. Amen." respond: "So mote it be." M rises to his feet, takes the by the right hand, and places and on the head and says:

"Mr (Name, or sometimes, Stranger!), in whom do you put your trust?" The candidate is prompted to reply: "In God." The WM continues: "Since in God you put your trust, your faith is well founded. Arise (assists candidate to rise), follow your conductor (SD) and fear no danger." The WM retires to his seat and, while the SD is leading the candidate once around the Lodge-room, he repeats a passage beginning: "Behold, how good and how pleasant it is for brethren to dwell together in unity!", while the candidate is conducted once around the Lodge room, at each of the stations in the East, South, and West, the officer that station gives one rap with his gavel as the candidate passes, still hoodwinked and with cable-tow, ending at the JW station in the South. He gives one rap, followed by one rap from the SD, then says: "Who comes here?" The SD replies: "Mr (Name) who has long been in darkness, and now seeks to be brought to light, and to receive a part in the rights and benefits of this Worshipful Lodge, erected to God, and dedicated to the Holy St John, as all brothers and fellows have done before."

There follows a dialogue relating to

the candidate being prepared and vouched for, etc. The JW says: "Since he is in possession of all these necessary qualifications, I will suffer him to pass on to the Senior Warden's station in the West." The SW passes him on to the WM, using the same words, and after the same dialogue as that used at the JW and SW stations, he asks: "From whence come you, and whither are you travelling?", to which the SD replies: "From the West, and travelling toward the East." The WM: "Why leave you the west and travel toward the east?" The SD replies: "In search of light." The WM then tells the SD: "Since light is the object of your search, you will reconduct the candidate, and place him in charge of the Senior Warden in the West, with my orders that he teach this candidate to approach the East, the place of light, by advancing with one upright, regular step to the first stop, the heel of his right placed in the hollow of his left foot, his body erect at the altar, before the Worshipful Master in the East."

The SD conducts the candidate to the SW, and passes the instructions of the Master. Leaving his seat, the SW approaches the candidate, faces him towards the WM and, having first brought him to within one pace of the altar, instructs him to make the step as demanded. The SW then informs the WM that: "The candidate is in order, and awaits your further will and pleasure." The WM then leaves his seat and approaches the candidate at the altar, He says: "Mr (Name), before you can be permitted to advance any farther in Masonry, it becomes my duty to inform you, that you must take upon yourself a solemn oath or obligation, appertaining to this degree, which I, as Master of this Lodge, assure you will not materially interfere with the duty that you owe to your God, yourself, family, country or neighbour. Are you willing to take such an oath?" The candidate replies: "I am."

The WM then says to the SW: "Brother Senior Warden, you will place the candidate in due form, which is by kneeling on his naked left knee, his right forming the angle of a square, his left hand supporting the Volume of Sacred Law, square, and compasses, his right hand resting thereon." The SW assists the candidate in adopting the due form, after which the WM tells the candidate: "Mr (Name), you are now in position for taking upon yourself the solemn oath of an Entered Apprentice Mason, and, if you have no objections still, you will say 'I', and repeat your name after me." The Master gives one rap with his gavel which is the signal for all present to assemble around the altar.

The candidate then makes his obligation, never to reveal any of the arts, parts or points of Ancient Free Masonry for which the penalty is to have "... my throat cut across, my tongue torn out by its roots, and my body buried in the rough sands of the sea, at low-water mark, where the tide ebbs and flows twice in twenty-four hours, should I ever knowingly violate this my Entered Apprentice obligation. So help me God, and keep me steadfast in the due performance of the same." In the Second Degree the penalty is "...of having my breast torn open, my heart plucked out, and placed on the highest pinnacle of the temple" (there are variations on this point), and the Third Degree, "...of having my body severed in two, my bowels taken from thence and burned to ashes, the ashes scattered before the four winds of heaven, ..."

After making the obligation, the candidate kisses the Volume of Sacred Law, is asked what he seeks and, on giving the reply "Light", the hoodwink is removed, and all gathered at the altar give the duegard of the degree. The cable-tow is then removed, as the new brother is "now held by a stronger tie." He is then told of the points of the compasses on the altar being hidden under the square, relating to his still being in the darkness of Masonry, and the significance of the Three Great Lights, and the Three Lesser Lights. There then follows while kneeling at the altar, the ritual act, and dialogue, of giving of the grip, pass and sign of the degree; which is acted out between the WM and SD, then repeated between the SD and JW, and the JW with the SW, who then passes the new brother on to the WM for the ceremonial presentation of a rolled up white apron. The WM delivers the charge to wear it with pleasure and

in honour of the fraternity. The brother is directed to return to the SD to be shown how to wear it in this degree.

The name of the grip is not given in plain speech but is spelled out, or given in syllables, in ritual form by each of the participants, alternately, saying one letter or syllable of the word. In the pass, Boaz, the name of the Entered Apprentice grip, the spelling ritually begins with 'A'; this is done to deter impostors.

After donning his apron, the new brother is brought before the WM who requests that a donation of a metal object is customary as a memento of the occasion. As he is unable, due to his being divested of all possessions before the ritual, he asks leave of the WM to pass outside, so that he may obtain his contribution. The WM refuses, keeping the new brother in suspense and confusion before telling him he is an object of charity, with little clothing, and no means to support himself. He then instructs the SD to conduct the brother to the Ante-room, where he will dress himself, have his apron tied, and return for further instruction. He is then placed at the WM's right, in the North-East of the Lodge room, where he is given the

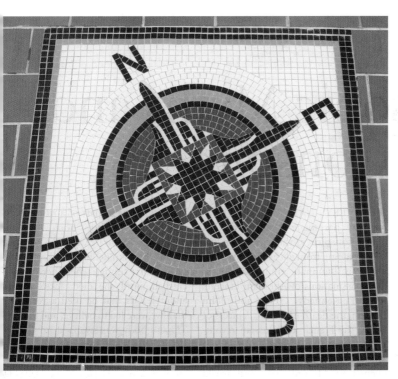

tools of his degree: an Entered Apprentice receives the twenty-four inch gauge and common gavel, Fellow Crafts receive the plumb, square and level and the Master Mason receives the trowel. There then follows a lecture on that degree, or additional ceremonial, that gives the Mason further knowledge or light. The Master Mason Degree includes a highly dramatic re-enactment of the killing of Hiram Abif, in which the initiate plays the part of Hiram.

Chapter 19

Masonic Myths and Conspiracies

THE VERY NATURE OF FREE-masonry has made it the subject of many conspiracy theories over the years, ranging from alleged involvement with the Illuminati, among others, in the assassinations of Abraham Lincoln, John F Kennedy (JFK) and John Lennon, the death of Diana, Princess of Wales, the French and Russian revolutions, Jack the Ripper, allegedly a Mason, who used a form of ritual killing likened to Masonic rite and world domination in the so-called New World Order.

David Icke, a former British television presenter, who once purported to be the son of God, claimed that Freemasons were involved in killing both JFK and Princess Diana as part of a ritual sacrifice. He claimed in his book *...and the truth shall set you free*, that the Masonic paramedic team deliberately kept Diana in the Paris tunnel, where her car had crashed, until she died. Icke's theory about JFK is that he died a year later than we were led to believe, and that J D Tippet's body was swapped for that of JFK, for the JFK autopsy. He also claims that Scottish Rite Freemasons erected an obelisk near Dealey Plaza, Dallas to celebrate the death of JFK.

Icke wrote in his book *The Biggest Secret* (pages 415-416): "Kennedy was assassinated in an outdoor temple of the Sun by initiates of the Brotherhood network including the Knights Templar, the Knights of Malta, the Order of St. John of Jerusalem, the Rosicrucians and the Freemasons." James Shelby Downard wrote: "Masonry does not believe in murdering a man in just any old way and in the JFK assassination it went to incredible lengths, and took great risks in order to make this heinous act correspond to the ancient fertility oblation [ie sacrifice] of the Killing of The King." Kennedy was shot just after noon when the Sun was 'most high'. In ancient times it was said that, when Hiram Abif was killed, "the Sun was 'most high', he was doing his father's work in the temple." None of these allegations have been substantiated

Others have claimed the United States was founded by Freemasons, who included Masonic symbols into US national seals of office, architecture, the

LEFT Albert Pike was extremely active in the affairs of the Freemasons

street layout of Washington D C, and famously, on the one dollar bill.

In more recent times, Freemasons have become more open, and have allowed the dissemination of information regarding some of their activities and beliefs. Previously, people asked questions about Freemasonry that were

RIGHT The Italian
nationalist Giuseppe
Mazzini joined the Craft

not answered, leaving many to believe that there might be an element of truth in some of the conspiracy theories. Those theories relating to political or religious conspiracies would be easiest to believe, and the hardest to defend, because of the rules of Freemasonry that ban the discussion of religion or politics.

Literature and, recently, the internet, have served as vehicles on which to publicise many of the conspiracy theories, often without providing any hard evidence, other than naming a Freemason with some connection to the subject under discussion. Conspiracy theories alleging or inferring the involvement of Freemasonry are not new. It has been claimed that The Jacobin Club, which was at the centre of the French revolutionary movement, was founded by prominent Freemasons. Other authors have implicated Freemasons as having played a key role in the instigation of the French Revolution, naming the Duke of Orleans, who was Grand Master of the Grand Orient Lodge of Freemasons, as being a significant person in the event.

Perhaps the most popular, and often repeated, conspiracy theory is the allegation that Freemasonry is a Jewish front for world domination. This charge has been levelled by diverse groups and individuals, and has been the subject of many books and films. It can be argued that there may be a case for the theory, bearing in mind that many world governments and corporate bodies are headed by Freemasons and, of these, there are many who are Jewish. Because Free-masonry requires a belief in a 'Supreme Being', it is open to all who hold that belief, whatever their religion. The prohibition of religious discussion within the Craft should provide assurance that there is no agenda for any religious group to control either Freemasonry or indeed, the world.

There is one widely reported, but unsubstan-tiated, instance of a letter said to have been written in 1871 by Albert Pike, a high-ranking American Freemason, to an Italian Freemason, Giuseppe Mazzini, a political activist, who as alleged to be a member of the Illuminati movement. In it, Pike outlined a plan for three world wars that would be necessary to bring about a One World Order. Anti-Masons claim the letter stated that the First World War must be brought about to overthrow the Russian Czars, and make the country an atheistic Communist state that would ultimately grow large enough to overthrow other governments, and destroy other religions. The Second War would be brought about to destroy Nazism, and ensure political Zionism was strong enough to enable creation of the state of Israel in Palestine, and also allow Communism to spread and strengthen. The Third War would ensure the mutual destruction of Islam and political Zionism, leading to social cataclysm in which both atheism and Christianity are rejected and destroyed, and the true light of Lucifer be brought into public view. History has placed some of these events in context.

Chapter 20

Nazis and Freemasonry

RIGHT German soldiers and civilians give the Nazi salute as thousands of books smoulder during one of the mass book-burnings

ADOLF HITLER ADMIRED SOME aspects of Freemasonry while, at the same time, despising it. He is quoted as saying: "...But there is one dangerous element and that is the element I have copied from them. They form a sort of priestly nobility. They have developed an esoteric doctrine not merely formulated, but imparted through the symbols and mysteries in degrees of initiation. The hierarchical organization and the initiation through symbolic rites, that is to say, without bothering the brain but by working on the imagination through magic and the symbols of a cult, all this has a dangerous element, and the element I have taken over. Don't you see that our party must be of this character...? An Order, that is what it has to be – an Order, the hierarchical Order of a secular priesthood... Ourselves or the Freemasons or the Church – there is room for one of the three and no more... We are the strongest of the three and shall get rid of the other two."

Hitler's attitude towards both the Jews and Freemasonry is apparent in the following extract attributed to him: "...and in Freemasonry, which has succumbed to him (the Jew) completely, he has an excellent instrument

with which to fight for his aims and put them across." His rise to power saw the dissolution of the ten Grand Lodges of Germany, and many members of the Order were incarcerated in concentration camps. An 'Anti-Masonic Exposition' in 1937 displayed Masonic books and objects, looted from the Lodges by the Gestapo. The Nazis continued the dissolution process in every country they occupied across Europe.

Chapter 21

Royalty and Prominent Freemasons

THERE HAS LONG BEEN A connection between the British monarchy and Freemasonry, dating back to George IV and William IV. Each of the three Kings of England who were Freemasons, and who reigned during the 20th century: Edward VII, Edward VIII, and George VI, maintained an active association with the Order subsequent to their respective accession to the throne. Some members of the Royal Family have held the highest office of the Order and several have been Grand Master of the United Grand Lodge of England (UGLE), including: Albert Edward, Prince of Wales (1874 – 1901), later King Edward VII, Prince Arthur, Duke of Connaught and Strathearn (1901 – 1939) and Prince George, Duke of Kent (1939 – 1942). The present Grand Master, since 1967, is Prince Edward, Duke of Kent. King Edward VIII, later The Prince Edward, Duke of Windsor (1894 – 1972) was initiated at the age of 14 years.

RIGHT King Edward VII dressed as Grand Master of the Freemasons, circa 1905

His Royal Highness, Prince Philip, Duke of Edinburgh was initiated into Navy Lodge No 2612 in 1952. Said to have been because of pressure from his future father-in-law, the then King George VI, there is no confirmed report of his active participation since the Accession of Queen Elizabeth II. Her Majesty, Queen Elizabeth II, is the Grand Patroness of Freemasonry but, being female, is not allowed into a Masonic Lodge. Prince Charles, Prince of Wales, has allegedly had pressure put upon him to become a Freemason: this he has refused to do, saying, "I do not wish to join any secret society."

It is said that only two US Presidents, Abraham Lincoln and John F Kennedy, were not Masons or members of affiliated bodies. Many prominent people in politics, religion, business, entertainment and sport belong to the Order.

Chapter 22

The Da Vinci Code

IN THE BOOK BY DAN BROWN, *The Da Vinci Code*, there are numerous references to Freemasonry. While there are some obvious similarities, many of the references and associations with Masonry have been refuted. On page 203 of the book, Brown makes reference to the use of keystones as a technique for building vaulted archways, and writes of the closely guarded secrets maintained by Masons that helped to make them wealthy.

He mentions The Royal Arch Degree and, two pages later, relates how, in the manner of most secret societies of which "The best known was the Masons (sic), Masons ascended to higher degrees by proving they could keep a secret, and by performing rituals and various tests of merit over the years. The tasks became progressively harder until they culminated in a successful candidate's induction as Thirty-second-degree Mason."

Brown also wrote of Hugo's *Hunchback of Notre Dame* and Mozart's *Magic Flute* both being filled with "Masonic symbolism and Grail secrets." Further on, he wrote of Rosslyn Chapel, near Edinburgh, telling of "...the richly carved stone that bore symbols of many religions and beliefs, as well as Masonic seals." There are many other Masonic references including that where Rosslyn is said to be

"...a copy of Solomon's Temple", and of the two stone pillars, Boaz and Jachin: "In fact, virtually every Masonic temple in the world has two pillars like these." Brown also has the female character, Sophie, saying "I've never been in a Masonic temple…".

The main character in the book, Dr Robert Langdon, is said to have been based on a real person, Dr Robert Lomas, himself a Freemason, who co-authored *The Hiram Key*, a worldwide best-selling book about the origins of Freemasonry.

Further information

For further information on Freemasonry there are many internet websites that may be accessed via a search engine such as Google. It must be made clear that some results returned by such a search may not bear totally accurate or unbiased information although they may contain related items of interest.

An official Masonic website is more likely to bear more accurate information on the subject. The website of the United Grand Lodge of England is a useful source. The URL is given here:

http://www.grandlodge-england.org/

Further information on Freemasonry and how to join can be obtained from:

The General Secretary
The United Grand Lodge of England
Freemasons' Hall
60 Great Queen Street
London WC2B 5AZ

Tel: 020 7831 9811
Fax: 020 7831 6021

Or, by asking anyone known to be a Mason, or by contacting a Lodge directly.

Further information on Freemasonry for women can be obtained from:

Order of Women Freemasons
27, Pembridge Gardens
London, NW2

The pictures in this book were provided courtesy of

GETTY IMAGES
www.gettyimages.com

SHUTTERSTOCK
www.shutterstock.com

PA PHOTOS
www.paphotos.com

Design and artwork by Jane Stephens

Image research by Ellie Charleston

Creative Director: Kevin Gardner

Published by Green Umbrella Publishing

Publishers: Jules Gammond and Vanessa Gardner

Written by David Greenland